STOCKING

®

FOOTBALL EDITION

By **S. Claus**
with help from **Jack Kreismer**

Red-Letter Press, Inc.

STOCKING STUMPERS- Football Edition
Copyright ©1997 Red-Letter Press, Inc.
ISBN: 0-940462-58-3
Printed in the United States of America

For information address Red-Letter Press, Inc.
P.O. Box 393, Saddle River, NJ 07458

ACKNOWLEDGMENTS

A Stocking Stumpers salute to Santa's "subordinate clauses":

Cover design and typography: **s.w.artz, inc.**

Illustrations: **Jack Kreismer, Sr.**

Editorial: **Ellen Fischbein and Geoff Scowcroft**

Contributors: **Angela Demers and Russ Edwards**

'Twas the Night Before Christmas
and I left the North Pole
to bring to your stocking
a fresh lump of coal;
But St. Nick's got heart
and your sins weren't voluminous,
so I brought you a gift
in lieu of bituminous;
Now since you've escaped
my long list of lumpers,
I've left you instead
Santa's favorite, Stocking Stumpers.
Merry Christmas!

S. Claus

FIRST THINGS FIRST

1. How much was a ticket to the first Super Bowl game?
2. Who was the first Heisman Trophy winner?
3. In 1995, Kendra Walker became the first female to participate in the finals of what NFL competition?
4. Who was the first black player selected to the Pro Football Hall of Fame?
5. Who was the first college varsity football player to become president of the United States?

ANSWERS

1. $6 (for the lowest priced ticket)

2. Jay Berwanger, 1935

3. The NFL Punt, Pass and Kick program - Walker finished second in the 12 year old age class. She passed the football 130 feet, punted it 76'6", and placekicked it 94'7".

4. Emlen Tunnell

5. Dwight Eisenhower, who was a starting halfback for the Military Academy of West Point in 1912

IN THE DRIVER'S SEAT

*The answers to each of the following questions contain the make
or model of an automobile.*

6. What do Alan Page, Pat Summerall, Lynn Swann and Drew Pearson
   have in common?

7. Where do the Lions play their home games?

8. Can you name the center who was chosen the outstanding player on the
   1934 Michigan squad and received pro football offers but opted for a
   career in politics instead?

9. With what team did Johnny Unitas wind up his career?

10. Larry Csonka and another running back made the 1972 Dolphins the first
    team in NFL history to have two 1,000-yard rushers. Do you know him?

ANSWERS

6. They all wore number 88
   (as in the Oldsmobile).

7. Pontiac, Michigan

8. Former U.S. President
   Gerald Ford

9. The San Diego Chargers

10. Mercury Morris

ON THE MOVE

Match the team with the former city in which it played.

11. St. Louis Rams   a) Baltimore
12. Baltimore Ravens   b) Dallas
13. Indianapolis Colts   c) Los Angeles
14. Washington Redskins   d) St. Louis
15. Kansas City Chiefs   e) Cleveland
16. Oakland Raiders   f) Boston
17. Arizona Cardinals   g) Anaheim

ANSWERS

11. G
12. E
13. A
14. F
15. B
16. C
17. D

TRUE OR FALSE

18. Quarterback Steve Young's great-great-great grandfather was baseball Hall of Fame pitching legend Cy Young.

19. In 1985, Miami Dolphins wide receiver Mark Duper went to court and legally changed his name to Mark Super Duper.

20. The first prime time Monday night football game was in 1966.

21. The quarterback's exclamation for the football snap stems from "Hut" as in football Hall of Famer Don "Hut"son who was involved in so many plays in early Green Bay Packer history.

ANSWERS

18. False - Young is the great-great-great grandson of Mormon leader Brigham Young.

19. True

20. True - but not on ABC-TV. On October 31, 1966, CBS televised a Monday night game in which the Cardinals defeated the Bears, 24-17. The announcers were Lindsey Nelson and Frank Gifford.

21. False - Football historians say that the "hut" stems from Army drills where the sergeant would count off "Hut-2-3-4".

PHRASE CRAZE

Santa's fond of brain teasers. Help him figure out what football phrases these items represent.

22. T
    O
    U
    C
    H

23. RETRAUQ

24. PAS_

25. REVERSE
    REVERSE

ANSWERS

22. Touchdown
23. Quarterback
24. Incomplete pass
25. Double reverse

PIGSKIN POTPOURRI

26. What Baptist preacher is known as the Minister of Defense?
27. Which college football team holds the record for most consecutive wins?
28. Only two players have won the Heisman Trophy, the NFL Player of the Year, and the Super Bowl MVP award. Who are they?
29. Four quarterbacks were named to the NFL's 75th Anniversary All-Time Team in 1994. How many can you name?
30. Former Dallas Cowboy running back Tony Dorsett holds a record which can be tied but never broken. What is it?

ANSWERS

26. Reggie White

27. The Oklahoma Sooners, coached by Bud Wilkinson, won 47 straight games from 1953-57.

28. Marcus Allen and Roger Staubach

29. Joe Montana, Johnny Unitas, Sammy Baugh and Otto Graham

30. A 99 yard touchdown run (against the Minnesota Vikings in 1993)

TUBE TEST

31. What former NFLer turned broadcaster proposed to his wife on national TV?

32. Can you name the former football commentator who was the only sportscaster ever to come in "most popular" and "least popular" in the same poll?

33. Which network televised the first Super Bowl game?
    a) ABC b) NBC c) CBS d) FOX

34. What football player was portrayed in the made for television movie *Brian's Song*?

35. Who sings the *Monday Night Football* theme song?

ANSWERS

31. Ahmad Rashad

32. Howard Cosell

33. B and C - NBC had the rights to the AFL games while CBS televised NFL contests before the two leagues merged. Both networks opted to carry the game.

34. Brian Piccolo

35. Hank Williams, Jr.

M&M's

The answers to each of these questions all have the initials M.M.

36. Who caught the longest touchdown pass in the history of the Pittsburgh Steelers?

37. He played for USC in 1925 and 1926, then changed his name and starred in flicks rather than football. Do you know him?

38. Who scored the first touchdown in the Super Bowl?

39. Who is the all-time leading rusher in the old All-America Football Conference?

40. He's among the top ten career scoring leaders in the NFL, a standout kicker from 1970 to 1986. Can you name him?

ANSWERS

36. None other than quarterback Mark Malone, an 88 yard pass from Terry Bradshaw

37. Marion Morrison (who changed his name to John Wayne)

38. Max McGee

39. Marion Motley

40. Mark Moseley

NAMES AND NUMBERS

Match the player with his retired uniform number

41. Dick Butkus	a) 44
42. Joe Schmidt	b) 74
43. Bob Griese	c) 51
44. Gale Sayers	d) 12
45. Pete Retzlaff	e) 40
46. Len Dawson	f) 56
47. Merlin Olsen	g) 16

ANSWERS

41. C
42. F
43. D
44. E
45. A
46. G
47. B

THREE'S A CROWD

Here's a trio of true or false stadium questions.

48. Which stadium has the largest capacity of any football venue in the country?

49. True or false: The weather was lousy and the attendance was worse when Washington State played San Jose State on November 12, 1955. A crowd of one showed up.

50. Giants Stadium is home to both the Jets and Giants. Who has drawn the largest crowd in the stadium's history?

ANSWERS

48. Michigan Stadium in Ann Arbor

49. True

50. Pope John Paul II, who said Mass there in October of 1995

TEASER TIMEOUT

It's time to take a break from the trivia. Try your hand at these brain teasers.

51. Before being injured early in the game, quarterback Troy Aikman threw five passes. All were incomplete, yet his passing percentage did not change. Why not?

52. Dan Marino can hurl a football that would stop in mid-flight, reverse direction and then return to him. How does he manage this?

53. Players have it- the Steelers and Eagles always, Cowboys and Packers never; although the Lions had it first, the Bills have it twice. What is it?

ANSWERS

51. It was opening day so Aikman's percentage was .000 going into the game and it remained just that.

52. He throws it up into the air.

53. The letter "l"

CONFERENCE CALL

Match the team with its college athletic conference.

54. Georgia Tech

55. Kansas State

56. Purdue

57. Arizona

58. Miami (Fla.)

59. Texas

60. Georgia

a) PAC-10

b) Southeastern Conference

c) Big East

d) Atlantic Coast Conference

e) Big Eight

f) Big Ten

g) Southwest Conference

ANSWERS

54. D
55. E
56. F
57. A
58. C
59. G
60. B

DEE-FENSE!

61. Who's the NFL's all-time sack leader?

62. What was the nickname of the defense of the undefeated 1972 Miami Dolphins?

63. Who's the only two-time winner of the Butkus award as the nation's outstanding (college) linebacker?

64. Who holds the NFL single season record for interceptions?

65. What defensive end played in the most consecutive games in the history of the NFL?

ANSWERS

61. Reggie White
62. The No Name Defense
63. Brian Bosworth of Oklahoma, 1985 and 1986
64. Dick "Night Train" Lane, 14
65. Jim Marshall, 282 games

GETTING THEIR KICKS

66. What NFL placekicking great was nicknamed "The Toe"?

67. Steve Little (Arkansas), Russell Erxleben (Texas) and Joe Williams (Wichita State) share the NCAA-I-A record for the longest field goal. How long?

68. What Iowa punter holds the NCAA-I-A single season record for the highest average, 49.8 yards per kick?

    a) Dave Jennings b) Ray Guy c) John Jett d) Reggie Roby

69. You be the ref: Chicago Bears placekicker Kevin Butler boots the ball through the uprights at Soldier Field but a gust of winds blows the ball back through them. Is it a field goal or not?

70. What placekicker/quarterback is the NFL's all-time scoring leader?

ANSWERS

66. Lou Groza

67. 67 yards

68. D

69. No - according to Section 5, Article 1C of the NFL's rulebook, "The entire ball must pass through the goal. In case wind or other forces cause it to return through the goal, it must have struck the ground or some object or person before returning."

70. George Blanda, 2,002 points

PIGSKIN POTPOURRI

71. The Cleveland Browns shut out the Baltimore Colts 27-0 in the 1964 NFL title game. The score at the half was: a) 27-0 b) 24-0 c) 3-0 d) 0-0

72. Who was the youngest inductee into the Pro Football Hall of Fame?

73. What is the Canadian Football League's version of the Super Bowl called?

74. What pro football Hall of Famer pitched in the big leagues and gave up two of Babe Ruth's then-record 60 homers in 1927?

75. Turner Field, which hosted the 1996 Olympics and is the new home of the Atlanta Braves, is one of three National League baseball stadiums that have never been the home of a pro football team. Can you name the others?

ANSWERS

71. D

72. Gale Sayers, 34, in 1977

73. The Grey Cup

74. Ernie Nevers

75. Coors Field (Denver)
    and Dodgers Stadium
    (Los Angeles)

PASSING FADS

*Listed below are the last names of quarterback/receiver combos. The letters are in
their proper order, but the names have been combined.
Your job is to separate them.*

Example- YROIUCNEG= Young and Rice

76. BCLEODATSOEES
77. MCAORTOERN
78. FBRAOOVRKSE
79. GGEORREEGEN
80. MAMCRIDUFNFIOE
81. HAARNDBAERSUGOHN

ANSWERS

76. Bledsoe and Coates
77. Moon and Carter
78. Favre and Brooks
79. George and Green
80. Marino and McDuffie
81. Harbaugh and Anderson

I-FORMATION

These clues all suggest last names which begin with the letter "I".

82. He was an All-Big Eight Conference defensive back in 1965 and 1966 for the Colorado Buffaloes but became a top performer in another sport - golf.

83. In 1972, this man traded his entire team, the Los Angeles Rams, to Carroll Rosenbloom for Rosenbloom's team, the Baltimore Colts.

84. Nicknamed "Pop", he was the last coach in Chicago Cardinals football history (in 1958 and 1959).

85. He owns the all-time career mark for catches and receiving yardage on the Dallas Cowboys.

ANSWERS

82. (Hale) Irwin
83. (Robert) Irsay
84. (Frank) Ivy
85. (Michael) Irvin

THREE ON A MATCH

86. What three old-line NFL teams joined the ten AFL teams in 1970 to form the American Football Conference?

87. Can you name the three Miami Dolphins who left the club after its second straight Super Bowl win to join the World Football League in 1975?

88. Who were the three men in the ABC broadcast booth for the first *Monday Night Football* game?

89. From 1982 to 1984, three straight Heisman Trophy winners chose to sign with the USFL. How many do you know?

90. In 1986, this player was drafted in three different sports. He was the #1 pick of Tampa Bay, a fourth-round pick of baseball's Kansas City Royals, and a fifth-round pick of the Continental Basketball Association's Savannah Spirits. Name him.

ANSWERS

86. The Browns, Colts, and Steelers

87. Larry Csonka, Jim Kiick and Paul Warfield

88. Keith Jackson, Howard Cosell
    and Don Meredith

89. Herschel Walker, Mike Rozier
    and Doug Flutie

90. Bo Jackson

MATCHMAKER, MATCHMAKER

See if you can pair up these couples who are, or were, an item.

91. Frank Gifford   a) Jane Russell
92. Terry Bradshaw   b) Joey Heatherton
93. Bob Waterfield   c) Kathie Lee Johnson
94. Mark Gastineau   d) Jo Jo Starbuck
95. Lance Rentzel   e) Brigitte Nielsen

ANSWERS

91. C
92. D
93. A
94. E
95. B

INITIALLY SPEAKING

In this quiz, the number on the left is based upon the first letters for words which are provided on the right.

Example: 10= Y. for a F.D. (Yards for a First Down)

96. 16= G. in an NFL R. S.
97. 22= P. on a F.F.
98. 2= P. for a S.
99. 160= W. of a F. F., in F
100. 16,726= Y. G. by W. P.

ANSWERS

96. Games in an NFL
    Regular Season

97. Players on a Football Field

98. Points for a Safety

99. Width of a Football Field, in Feet

100. Yards Gained by Walter Payton

LAUGH-IN TIMEOUT

See if you can answer some of Santa's favorite football groaners, provided by resident North Pole jokester Henny Elfman.

101. How do you keep a Bear out of your front yard?

102. Why did the coach send a monster into the game?

103. How much does corn cost at a Tampa Bay game?

104. What do St. Louis players do to fall asleep?

105. What is the favorite drink of the Cowboy Cheerleaders?

ANSWERS

101. Put up goalposts
102. Because his team needed a field ghoul
103. A buc-an-ear
104. They count rams.
105. Root beer

WHO SAID IT?

106. "They boo for a living in those places (Cleveland and Cincinnati fans).
We played on Christmas Eve and they even booed Santa Claus."
a) Jerry Glanville b) Don Shula c) Rich Kotite d) Richie Allen

107. "It's a game (football) in which you can feel a clean hatred
for your opponent."
a) Mike Ditka b) Woody Hayes c) Ronald Reagan d) Ronald McDonald

108. "The man who complains about the way the ball bounces is likely the
one who dropped it."
a) Jerry Rice b) Jack Tatum c) Dan Marino d) Lou Holtz

109. "One loss is good for the soul. Too many losses is not good for the coach."
a) Tom Landry b) John Madden c) Knute Rockne d) Bear Bryant

110. "When you win, you're an old pro. When you lose, you're an old man."
a) George Blanda b) Joe Namath c) Charlie Conerly d) Charlie McCarthy

ANSWERS

106. A (Glanville was the Houston
     Oilers coach at the time.)

107. C

108. D

109. C

110. C

PIGSKIN POTPOURRI

111. Who was the first congressman to be inducted into the
   Pro Football Hall of Fame?

112. Who was the "other" end when Don Hutson played for Alabama?
   a) Sammy Baugh b) Paul Brown c) Bear Bryant d) Bryant Gumbel

113. Name the only father and son to play quarterback in the NFL.

114. Can you name the current and previous voice of NFL highlight films?

115. You may remember that Tom Dempsey kicked a record-setting 63 yard
   field goal in 1970, but do you know whose record he broke?

ANSWERS

111. Former Seattle Seahawks wide receiver Steve Largent, the Republican U.S. Representative from Oklahoma, in 1995

112. C

113. Jack and Jeff Kemp

114. Harry Kalas and John Facenda, respectively

115. Baltimore Colts placekicker Bert Rechichar's 56-yarder in 1953

NICKNAMES

Santa is making his list (and checking it twice). Help St. Nick match each quarterback with his nickname.

116. Roger Staubach
117. Ron Jaworski
118. Terry Bradshaw

119. Bob Waterfield
120. Fran Tarkenton
121. Ken Stabler

a) The Snake
b) The Rifle
c) The Artful Dodger
d) The Scrambler
e) Ozark Ike
f) The Polish Rifle

ANSWERS

116. C
117. F
118. E
119. B
120. D
121. A

BROTHERLY LOVE

122. Walter Payton's brother was a running back and kick returner in the NFL, for four teams over a five year period. What's his first name?

123. Doug Flutie's brother, Darren, also played for Boston College. What position?

124. Phil Olsen was a defensive lineman for the Rams from 1971 to 1974. His brother Orrin was a center for the K.C. Chiefs in 1976. Can you think of the third brother who played in the NFL?

125. Brothers Joey, Keith, Ross and Jim all played in the NFL. What is their last name?

126. He was a kick returner for the Colts. His brother, Dale, played baseball for the New York Yankees. So did his father. Do you know him?

ANSWERS

122. Eddie

123. Wide receiver

124. Merlin Olsen, a Hall of Fame
     lineman for the Rams

125. Browner

126. Tim Berra

BOWL GAMES

127. What stadium hosts the Sugar Bowl?

128. True or false: The oldest college bowl game is the Orange Bowl.

129. Five colleges have won each of the "big four" bowl games- the Rose Bowl, Sugar Bowl, Cotton Bowl and Orange Bowl. How many can you name?

130. What was the Citrus Bowl formerly called?

ANSWERS

127. The Superdome, in New Orleans

128. False - it's the Rose Bowl, first played in 1902.

129. Alabama, Georgia, Georgia Tech, Notre Dame and Penn State

130. The Tangerine Bowl

BROACHING COACHING

131. Of all college coaches with 100 victories or more, who has the best winning percentage?

132. Coaching legends Tom Landry and Vince Lombardi worked together as assistant coaches from 1954 to 1958 for what team?

133. Who is the only college coach to have won more than 400 games?

134. Can you name the coach who led Notre Dame to four national championships from 1943 to 1949?

135. In 1977, after the Tampa Bay Bucs had lost their 26th straight game, a reporter asked the coach what he thought about his team's execution. He responded, "I'm in favor of it." Who was the coach?

ANSWERS

131. Knute Rockne, .881 (105-12-5)
132. The New York Giants
133. Eddie Robinson
134. Frank Leahy
135. John McKay

A RUSH ORDER

136. Who's the only NFL player to rush for 100 yards in 11 straight games?

137. Who was the first NFL player to lead the NFL in rushing in his first three seasons?

138. Who's the all-time leading rusher in college football history?

139. Jim Brown holds the NFL rushing record with an average of 5.2 yards per carry. In college, he was an All-American in football and in another sport. Do you know it?

140. Who holds the NFL rushing record for most yards in a single season?

ANSWERS

136. Marcus Allen
137. Earl Campbell
138. Tony Dorsett, 6,082 yards
139. Lacrosse
140. Eric Dickerson, 2,105 yards

THE ONE AND ONLY

141. Who's the only Super Bowl MVP to become an NFL head coach?

142. Who's the only member of the College Football, Pro Football and Major League Baseball Halls of Fame?

143. Who's the only man to coach an NFL team and manage a Major League baseball club?

144. Who's the only man to win an Olympic Gold Medal, play in a baseball World Series, and be elected to the Pro Football Hall of Fame?

145. Can you name the only NFL team to play its home games in New York?

ANSWERS

141. Bart Starr

142. Cal Hubbard

143. Hugo Bezdek, who managed the Pittsburgh Pirates from 1917 to 1919 and coached the Cleveland Rams in 1937 and 1938.

144. Jim Thorpe

145. The Buffalo Bills (The Giants and Jets both play their home games in East Rutherford, N.J.)

TEASER TIMEOUT

Help yourself to another eggnog and try your hand at these three teasers.

146. Pigskin Pete, the prognosticator, claims he can tell the score of any football game before it even starts. How is it that he's accurate at least 99% of the time?

147. Take the number of Super Bowls the Packers have won, multiply that amount by the number of schools in the Big Ten, divide that by the number of offensive or defensive players on a football team, and multiply that by the number of times Joe Namath was selected as an All-American while at Alabama.

    And the answer is...

148. Bubba Booth was bragging about his local flag football team. He said, "Six of our guys scored touchdowns. We won 42-0 and not a single man crossed the goal line." How can this be?

ANSWERS

146. Since the score of any football game before it starts is always zero to zero, Pete wouldn't have too tough a time zeroing in on it.

147. The Packers have won two Super Bowls, there are 11 teams in the Big Ten, there are also eleven players on the field from one team at any given time, and Joe Namath was never selected as an All-American so the answer is 0.

148. Every one of Bubba's teammates was married.

TRUE OR FALSE

149. A high school football game is 48 minutes.

150. NFL uprights are 25 feet apart.

151. The single sporting event which draws the biggest crowd each year is the Super Bowl.

152. The date on which New Orleans was officially named the site of a new NFL franchise was All Saints Day, November 1, 1966.

153. Seven officials work a pro football game.

154. No pro football figure has ever been selected *Sports Illustrated* Sportsman of the Year.

155. Until 1917, the Rose Bowl was called the Pasadena Bowl.

ANSWERS

149. True

150. False - they are 18 feet, 6 inches apart.

151. False - it's the Tour de France bicycle race which annually draws more than ten million fans.

152. True

153. True - the referee, umpire, head linesman, line judge, back judge, side judge and field judge

154. False - there have been many; most recently, Don Shula (1993) and Joe Montana (1990).

155. True

KEEPING UP WITH THE JONESES

As the above suggests, the last name is Jones. What's the first name?

156. He was a defensive lineman for the Cowboys who had a brief stint as a professional boxer, undefeated in six bouts in 1979.

157. He was one of the Rams "Fearsome Foursome".

158. On December 15, 1974, this Colts quarterback set a record by completing 17 passes in a row against the Jets.

159. He's the owner of the Dallas Cowboys.

160. A linebacker out of Florida State, he was the Jets top draft pick in 1993.

ANSWERS

156. Ed "Too Tall" Jones
157. David "Deacon" Jones
158. Bert Jones
159. Jerry Jones
160. Marvin Jones

PIGSKIN POTPOURRI

161. Who set the national high school record by returning four kickoffs for touchdowns in a single game in 1951? (Hint: He set a Major League Baseball record ten years later.)

162. What do tight end Keith Jackson, running back Roger Craig, Army's "Mr. Outside", Glenn Davis, and kickoff returner Tim Brown share in common?

163. True or False: A stimpmeter is used to measure the spiral of a thrown football.

164. Where did Jim Thorpe go to college?

165. What was RFK Stadium, the former home of the Washington Redskins, originally called?

ANSWERS

161. Roger Maris, who broke Babe Ruth's record with 61 homers in 1961

162. The same name as other sports figures- Keith Jackson is also a sports commentator; Roger Craig was also a baseball pitcher and manager; Glenn Davis was also a Houston Astros baseball player; Tim Brown was also an Eagles running back.

163. False - named for Ed Stimpson, who developed it in 1935, a stimpmeter is used in golf to measure the speed of the greens on a golf course.

164. Carlisle Institute

165. D.C. Stadium

TURF 'N TURF

166. Which one of these college stadiums has artificial turf?
    a) Stanford Stadium b) Beaver Stadium
    c) Spartan Stadium d) Ohio Stadium

167. By what name do the people of New Orleans refer to the turf of the Superdome?

168. What is a foot injury caused by artificial turf commonly called?

169. Was the first Super Bowl game played on artificial or natural turf?

170. Which one of these stadiums had its original artificial turf replaced by natural grass?
    a) Lambeau Field b) Arrowhead Stadium c) Joe Robbie Stadium
    d) Veterans Stadium

ANSWERS

166. C (home of Michigan State)

167. Mardi Grass

168. Turf toe

169. Natural (at the L.A. Memorial Coliseum) - the first to
     be played on artificial surface was Super Bowl V
     in New Orleans.

170. B (home of the Kansas City Chiefs)

AUTHOR! AUTHOR!

Match the football book with the author.

171. Jack Tatum

172. George Plimpton

173. Dan Jenkins

174. John Madden

175. Vince Lombardi

a) *One Knee
   Equals Two Feet*

b) *Run for
   Daylight*

c) *They Call me
   Assassin*

d) *Semi-Tough*

e) *Paper Lion*

ANSWERS

171. C
172. E
173. D
174. A
175. B

THE SUPER BOWL

176. Do you know the first head coach to take two different teams to the Super Bowl?

177. Speaking of coaches, how about the first one to both win and lose a Super Bowl game?

178. Who played in Super Bowls in three decades?

179. What was the Super Bowl first called - and who coined the term "Super Bowl"?

180. What city has played host to the most Super Bowls?

ANSWERS

176. Don Shula

177. Hank Stram

178. Gene Upshaw- 1968, 1977 and 1981

179. It was first called "The AFL-NFL Championship Game". It wasn't until Super Bowl III (after the two leagues merged) that it was referred to as "The Super Bowl". The term was coined by K.C. Chiefs owner Lamar Hunt.

180. New Orleans, 8

FOOTBALL FEMALES

181. Marge Schott is to baseball as who is to football?

182. Who said, "If a man watches three football games in a row, he should be declared legally dead?"
   a) Erma Bombeck b) Lily Tomlin c) Carol Burnett

183. Who was the first female co-host of CBS-TV football broadcasts?

184. Who was the first woman play-by-play announcer for a network television NFL game?

185. Who said, "The reason woman don't play football is because eleven of them would never wear the same outfit in public?"
   a) Rita Rudner b) Phyllis Diller c) Jane Fonda

ANSWERS

181. Georgia Frontiere (Frontiere, owner of the Rams, and Schott, who owns baseball's Reds, are the only female owners in football and baseball.)

182. A

183. Phyllis George

184. Gayle Sierens, on December 27, 1987, was the play-by-play announcer for the Seahawks-Chiefs game on NBC-TV.

185. B

THE HEISMAN

186. As a freshman at the University of Georgia, I was third in Heisman Trophy voting. As a sophomore, I was second. In my junior year, I won the trophy. Who am I?

187. True or false: Floyd Little was the first black player to win the Heisman.

188. What Heisman Trophy winner went on to a career in the NBA?

189. What was the Heisman Trophy first called?

190. Who's the only two-time winner of the Heisman Trophy?

ANSWERS

186. Herschel Walker

187. False - fellow Syracuse alumnus Ernie Davis was first, in 1961.

188. Charlie Ward, Heisman winner in 1993

189. It was dubbed the DAC Trophy when first presented in 1935 by the Downtown Athletic Club of New York. A year later, it was renamed following the death of DAC athletic director and former college coach John Heisman.

190. Archie Griffin

TRIVIQUATION

Test your math and your sports wits here. Fill in the number portion of answers suggested by the clues and then perform the arithmetic to solve the Triviquation.

191. Marino record TD passes in a season .... _____

192. Little and Brown uniform # at Syracuse .... - _____

193. # of NFL teams in Florida ....**x** _____

194. Points for a safety ....÷ _____

195. Nevers' single game rushing TD record ....**=** _____

ANSWERS

191. 48
192. 44
193. 3
194. 2
195. 6

AND THE WINNER IS...

Match the college rivalry with the prize.

196. Minnesota-Michigan   a) The Axe
197. Texas-Oklahoma   b) The Wooden Beer Stein
198. Clemson-South Carolina   c) The Dog Collar
199. Idaho-Montana   d) Little Brown Jug
200. Florida-U. of Miami   e) The Cowboy Hat
201. California-Stanford   f) The Tea Cup
202. Wichita-Wichita St.   g) The Seminole War Canoe

ANSWERS

196. D
197. E
198. F
199. B
200. G
201. A
202. C

LAUGH-IN TIMEOUT #2

Here are some more groaners from Santa's sidekick, Henny Elfman.

203. Why was the college quarterback the sole member of the team
     to graduate?
204. What was the Atlanta NFLer who drank only tea at the shopping
     center called?
205. How many Jets does it take to screw in a light bulb?
206. What do a lousy team and an atheist have in common?
207. What does Notre Dame coach Lou Holtz write on his Christmas cards?

ANSWERS

203. He was the only one who could pass.

204. The mall-teas Falcon

205. Two - the other one recovers the fumble.

206. Neither has a prayer on Sunday.

207. "Irish you a Merry Christmas."

THREE-PETE

Three Petes are the solutions to the following clues.

208. He was the first of the soccer-style kickers in pro football, breaking in with the Buffalo Bills in 1964.

209. His uniform number 44 was retired by the Philadelphia Eagles.

210. His first name is actually Alvin. He was a publicist and GM who never petered out for the Los Angeles Rams, but you know him better from another position he held in the NFL.

ANSWERS

208. Pete Gogolak
209. Pete Retzlaff
210. Former NFL commissioner Pete Rozelle

PIGSKIN POTPOURRI

211. Who's the only member of the Pro Football Hall of Fame to have been born in Italy?
    a) Lou Groza   b) Lou Nomellini   c)Vince Lombardi   d) Y.A. Tittlini

212. What company manufactures footballs for the NFL?

213. In what melodious fashion is Father Michael Shea connected with the annals of Notre Dame football?

214. To be or not to be: What does William Shakespeare have to do with the history of the Pittsburgh Steelers?

215. What did the town of Ismay, Montana, become in 1993?

ANSWERS

211. B (Nomellini was a two-way star at offensive and defensive tackle for the 49ers.)

212. Wilson

213. He wrote Notre Dame's *Victory March* (the song that starts out, "Cheer, cheer for old Notre Dame") in 1909.

214. He was the Steelers' very first pick in the first NFL draft in 1936.

215. The town changed its name to Joe, Montana, in honor of the former quarterback.

THE HALL OF NAMES

216. What is Weeb Ewbank's (the only coach to win an AFL and an NFL championship) first name?

217. Lance Alworth was the first AFL player selected to the Pro Football Hall of Fame. By what deerlike nickname was the former wide receiver known?

218. By what names were the Jets, Bears, and Eagles formerly known?

219. What football team was named for its owner and former coach?

220. What was the first name of Red Grange?

ANSWERS

216. Wilbur

217. Bambi

218. The Titans, Decatur Staleys, and
     Yellow Jackets, respectively

219. The Cleveland Browns
     (for Paul Brown)

220. Harold

A PASS AND A PRAYER

221. In the 1982 NFC championship, Dwight Clark caught a TD pass, giving the 49ers a 28-27 win over the Cowboys. This play is known simply as what?

222. "The Immaculate Reception" was a fourth down, fourth quarter desperation pass from Steeler quarterback Terry Bradshaw to whom?

223. A 49-yard touchdown pass with no time left on the clock enabled Boston College to upend Miami, 47-45, in 1984. What Heisman winner threw the pass and, for extra credit, who caught it?

224. In a 1975 NFC divisional playoff game, Roger Staubach threw what has become known as "The Hail Mary" pass. Who caught it?

225. In Super Bowl VII, when Miami defeated Washington 14-7, what Dolphin placekicker had his field goal attempt blocked, recovered the ball, then frantically attempted a pass (later ruled a fumble) which was gobbled up and returned for a touchdown by the Redskins Mike Bass?

ANSWERS

221. "The Catch"

222. Franco Harris - the pass, intended for Frenchy Fuqua, was misthrown but miraculously wound up in Harris' hands, giving the Steelers a 13-7 AFC divisional playoff win over the Raiders in 1972.

223. Doug Flutie was the quarterback, Gerard Phelan the receiver

224. Drew Pearson - the catch made the Cowboys 17-14 winners over the Vikings.

225. Garo Yepremian

ALMA MATER

Match the player with the college he attended.

226. Steve McNair   a) Miami (Fla)

227. Jerry Rice   b) Oklahoma St.

228. Warren Sapp   c) Auburn

229. Mike Ditka   d) Alcorn St.

230. Barry Sanders   e) Virginia Tech

231. Bruce Smith   f) Mississippi Valley

232. Bo Jackson   g) BYU

233. Jim McMahon   h) Pittsburgh

ANSWERS

226. D
227. F
228. A
229. H
230. B
231. E
232. C
233. G

PIGSKIN POTPOURRI

234. What is coincidental about the birthplace of pro football Hall-of-Famers Alan Page and John Hannah?

235. Who is the only man to play in a World Series and in a Super Bowl game?

236. Can you name the onetime NFL rushing champion who had a brother who won a Major League batting crown?

237. Who's the only man to play on a national championship team, coach a team to the national collegiate championship and be an NFL Super Bowl champion coach?

238. What's the only team to play in the Super Bowl in the sixties, seventies and eighties?

239. Who's the first player ever drafted by the Baltimore Ravens?

240. Yelbert and Abraham were the given names of what Hall-of-Famer?

ANSWERS

234. They were both born in Canton, Ohio, the home of the Pro Football Hall of Fame.

235. Deion Sanders, in baseball for the Braves and in football for the 49ers and Cowboys

236. Ron Johnson (1972) had a brother, Alex, who won the American League batting crown (1971).

237. Jimmy Johnson, who played for Arkansas in 1964, coached the Miami Hurricanes to a national title in 1987, and guided the Dallas Cowboys to two Super Bowl wins.

238. The Raiders

239. Offensive lineman Jonathan Ogden

240. Y.A. Tittle

A MAN FOR ALL SEASONS

241. He was a gold medalist in the 1964 Olympics and a wide receiver for the Dallas Cowboys from 1965-1974. Can you name him?

242. Can you name the footballer who was on the 1992 U.S. Olympic bobsled team?

243. You know me better as a baseball club owner but, by George, I was an assistant football coach at Purdue in the fifties. Who am I?

244. Who was the first man to play in an NFL Pro Bowl Game and in a Major League Baseball All-Star Game?

245. He played for the San Francisco 49ers and the Boston Red Sox, where he was the only player to ever pinch-hit for Ted Williams. Who is he?

246. He was boxer "Apollo Creed" in the *Rocky* films and was a linebacker for the Oakland Raiders in 1970 and 1971. Do you know him?

ANSWERS

241. "Bullet" Bob Hayes
242. Herschel Walker
243. George Steinbrenner
244. Bo Jackson
245. Carroll Hardy
246. Carl Weathers

'TIS THE SEASON

247. It was on Christmas Day in 1971 when Santa got a chance to sit back and relax after making the usual hectic rounds the night before. He decided to take in an NFL playoff football game between the Miami Dolphins and the Kansas City Chiefs. Little did he know that he was watching a record-breaking contest. Do you know what it was?

248. What do former footballers Ken Stabler and Larry Csonka share in common?

249. The Green Bay Packers won the NFL championship on New Year's Eve and New Year's Day in 1967. Can you explain this?

ANSWERS

247. It was the longest game in NFL history. The outcome wasn't decided until the Dolphins' Garo Yepremian kicked a 37-yard field goal more than 22 minutes into overtime to give Miami a 27-24 victory.

248. They share the same birthday, December 25th.

249. On January 1, 1967, the Packers defeated Dallas 34-27 to earn the right to represent the NFL versus the AFL (before the two leagues merged). Then, on January 31, 1967, the Packers edged the Cowboys again, 21-17, to win the NFL championship.

THE TWELVE DAYS OF CHRISTMAS?

250. Do you know the winning team's score in a forfeited football game, the number of commissioners of the NFL since 1960, Joe Montana's uniform number while at Notre Dame, the number of seams on a pro football, the Super Bowl in which Cowboy linebacker Chuck Howley became the only MVP to be from the losing team, what number draft pick Jim Brown was in 1956, the width of a football (in inches), the collegiate single game record number of touchdowns Illinois running back Howard Griffith scored in 1990, the total number of players the L.A. Rams traded to the Chicago Cardinals in 1959 for running back Ollie Matson, the height (in feet) of a goalpost crossbar, the number of teams in the Big Ten, and the number worn by the winning quarterback in every Super Bowl from 1972 to 1980?

ANSWERS

250. 1, 2, 3, 4, 5, 6, 7, 8, 9, 10, 11, and 12.
    If you took into consideration the subject matter
    (The Twelve Days of Christmas?), you probably realized
    this was a gift from Santa.